ROUJO-K WILSON

MULTIPLE STREAMS OF INCOME

A Guide

No parts of this book shall be reproduced, copied, published without the consent of the author.
Copyright © 2023
Roujo-k Wilson
Printed by Crystal Evans Book House

Email: RoujokWilson@gmail.com for further consultation

"For you Iyara - The catalyst to my success."

Table of Content

- Multiple Streams of Income: The Key to Financial Freedom ------------- 1
- What are Multiple Streams of Income? ---- 2
- Multiple Streams of Income: Leveraging Your Existing Skillset ----------------- 3
- **Stream #1:** Instruction/Training ------- 4
  - Bonus --------------------- 6
- **Stream #2:** DIY End Product ---------- 8
- **Stream #3:** Sell Necessary Equipment & Supplies ------------------------- 9
- **Stream #4:** Complementing Products -- 10
  - Bonus --------------------- 11
- **Stream #5:** Capitalizing Your Space ---- 17
  - Bonus --------------------- 18
- **Stream #6:** Personalized Swag & Clothes   21
- **Stream #7:** Social Media ------------ 22
  - Bonus --------------------- 23
- **Stream #8:** Brand Partnership -------- 25
- Bonus Streams to Earn More Money ----- 26
- Jamaican Bonus Business Ideas -------- 28
- **Bonus Section:** Tools for Entrepreneurs - 32

Multiple Streams of Income: The Key to Financial Freedom

Financial freedom is a term thrown around often, but what does it really mean? At its core, financial freedom is the ability to control your finances without relying on one source of income. The ultimate goal is to have more than one avenues for financing your dreams, which is where the concept of multiple income streams comes in. Multiple income streams are critical in today's fast-paced world, where the economy is constantly changing, and job security is no longer guaranteed.

What are Multiple Streams of Income?

Multiple streams of income refer to having several sources of income, which can come from various channels. It's not just about making more money but not relying on one source of income. This means that if one source of income dries up, you'll still have other sources of income to fall back on. With multiple streams of income, you can have financial stability, regardless of the ups and downs of the economy.

Multiple Streams of Income: Leveraging Your Existing Skillset

Regardless of your current profession or skillset, several income streams can leverage your existing skills. You don't have to start from scratch or learn a new skill; as long as you have a passion for what you do, there's always a way to turn it into a profitable business. Here are eight primary streams of income that you can explore:

Stream #1: Instruction/

Instruction and training are great ways to monetize your skills and expertise. By offering your knowledge to others, you can create a second stream of income that complements your primary career. Whether you prefer self-paced instruction or hands-on training, there are many options for you to explore.

Self-paced instruction is a great way to reach a broad audience. You can create a video course and post it on platforms like Teachable or YouTube. This is an excellent option for those who are comfortable with video production and have the necessary equipment. By creating a course, you can reach a large audience and offer your expertise in a format that is accessible and convenient for your students. To maximize your earnings, ensure that you are offering your courses on multiple platforms such as Udemy, Skillshare, and Kajabi. Additionally, create e-books that complement your courses or can be sold separately to individuals who prefer a book format. These e-books can provide in-depth explanations, step-by-step instructions, and additional resources, enhancing the learning experience for your audience.

Regardless of your format, offering instruction and training is a great way to earn a second income stream. By sharing your knowledge, you can help others while generating additional income. Whether you're a photographer, nail technician, phone repair technician, or have another area of expertise, there is likely a way for you to monetize your skills through instruction and training.

If you prefer hands-on instruction, offering in-person classes can be a rewarding option. This option is ideal for those prefer a more immersive and personalized learning environment. For example, whether you're a skilled nail technician offering in-person classes on acrylic application or a phone repair technician teaching the intricacies of device repair, hands-on training can be a valuable experience for both you and your students.

BONUS

1. If you have a knack for teaching and connecting with younger audiences, targeting 5th and 6th formers can be a rewarding experience. Consider creating courses tailored to their interests and developmental needs, ensuring they are both educational and engaging. These courses will equip students with the practical skills needed to go straight into the work force.

2. College life often comes with financial challenges, making it essential for students to find innovative ways to earn extra income. Market your courses to college students who can leverage your course, develop their expertise and begin offering service to their peers.

3. Moving to a new country for education can be an exciting yet challenging experience. Students who are planning to move abroad often seek ways to support themselves financially while adapting to their new surroundings. By offering skills training courses tailored to their needs, you can provide them with a potential hustle that allows them to earn money while immersing themselves in their new environment.

4. Be sure to leverage technology and other resources. Harnessing the power of technology can significantly streamline the course creation process. Artificial intelligence tools like ChatGPT can assist you in designing and refining your course content, ensuring it is comprehensive, engaging, and impactful. Additionally, platforms like Fiverr and Upwork provide access to a pool of talented contractors who can help you design your course materials and write accompanying e-books. By leveraging these resources, you can create high-quality educational products that resonate with your target audience.

5. To give you a head start, here are a few course ideas:

- Introduction to Culinary Arts
- Everyday Makeup for Beginners
- Introduction to Event Planning
- Introduction to Photography and editing
- Introduction to Cosmetology

Stream #2: DIY End Product

Creating a DIY end product is a great way to supplement your income and tap into a new market. You can provide value and make money from your skills and knowledge by offering a product that others can use. When choosing a product to sell, consider what you enjoy doing and what you are good at.

For example, if you're a nail technician, you can create a line of press-on nails that people can use to create a salon-quality look at home. If you're an accountant, you can create an app or software that helps people manage their finances. By selling a product you have made, you can build a brand and offer value to others while earning a second income stream.

You can also consider offering personalized products that cater to specific customers. For example, if you're a photographer, you can provide custom presets for different photography styles such as portrait, landscape, or street photography

By creating a DIY end product, you have the potential to reach a wider audience and build a new revenue stream. With the rise of e-commerce and digital platforms, getting your products in front of potential customers has never been easier. Consider your skills and expertise, and find ways to turn them into a profitable product.

Stream #3: Sell Necessary Equipment & Supplies

By offering necessary equipment and supplies, professionals in various careers can help their peers with the tools they need to succeed and make an additional income stream. By understanding the needs of their target audience, professionals can curate a selection of products that cater to their specific requirements. This not only saves time for the customers but also helps them build a reputation as a one-stop shop for their customers

For instance, photographers selling cameras and backdrops can also provide personalized recommendations based on their experiences and insights. They can become trusted advisors to their customers, increasing the likelihood of repeat business and building a loyal customer base. Similarly, nail technicians who sell UV machines and gel polish can also provide support and troubleshooting tips to help their customers achieve their desired results.

By capitalizing on the demand for this necessary equipment and supplies, professionals can create a steady income stream and establish a reputation as a reliable and knowledgeable provider of essential tools for their industry.

Stream #4: Complementing Products

Supplementing your main income stream by offering related products or services to your clients and customers can be an innovative and efficient way to increase your revenue. This strategy provides you with a secondary source of income and demonstrates your commitment to providing a comprehensive and satisfying experience for your clients.

For instance, if you're a photographer, you can offer your clients picture frames, print images, or even rental props. These products complement your photography services and can provide a convenient one-stop-shop experience for your clients. Similarly, a phone repair technician can sell phone cases, offering added protection for the device they just repaired. Farmers can expand their business by selling reusable grocery bags or commercial-grade juicing machines, tapping into the growing demand for farm-to-table produce and health-conscious consumers. An accountant can offer business registration services to help new entrepreneurs set up their businesses, making starting a new business more streamlined and efficient.

By offering related products or services, you can expand your business and show your clients that you are dedicated to providing them with a comprehensive and fulfilling experience.

1. For a Fitness Trainer:

- Workout apparel tailored to different exercise routines.
- Nutritional supplements to support fitness goals.
- Fitness equipment such as resistance bands or dumbbells for home work outs.
- Fitness trackers or smartwatches to monitor progress.
- Healthy recipe books or meal planning guides for a well-rounded approach.
- Workout accessories like gym bags or water bottles.
- Meal prep services for convenience and meal management.
- Stopwatch or interval timers for timing workouts and tracking progress.
- Fitness assessment tools, such as body composition analysers or measuring tapes.

BONUS

In previous sections we explored ways to generate additional streams of income while establishing yourself as a comprehensive and trusted resource for your customers and industry peers. This section explores examples of DIY end products, necessary equipment and supplies, as well as complementary items that can be sold online through various platforms including online stores in order to maximize your reach.

2. For a Phone Repair Store:

- Phone and tablet cases for personalization and protection.
- Bluetooth speakers and headphones for an enhanced audio experience.
- Portable power banks and chargers for on-the-go convenience.
- Customizable phone case kits, allowing customers to design their own unique cases.
- Replacement parts and components, including screens, batteries, and connectors.
- Anti-static gloves and mats for safe handling of electronic components.

3. For a Coffee Shop:

- Gourmet coffee beans or blends for customers to enjoy at home.
- Coffee mugs and tumblers featuring your brand or unique designs.
- Pastry or snack items like cookies or granola bars that complement your coffee offerings.
- Coffee brewing equipment, such as espresso machines or coffee grinders.
- Point-of-sale systems and cash registers tailored for coffee shops.

4. For a Beauty Salon:

- Hair care products (shampoo, conditioner, styling products) for at-home maintenance.
- Nail polish and manicure/pedicure accessories for self-care.
- Skincare products (face masks, serums, moisturizers) to promote healthy skin.
- Salon-grade hair styling tools, including hairdryers, curling irons, and straighteners.
- Salon furniture, such as styling chairs, manicure tables, and hairdressing stations.

5. For a Home Cleaning Service:

- Cleaning supplies and tools for customers to maintain cleanliness.
- Organizational products like storage bins or closet organizers.
- Cleaning carts and organizers for convenient storage and transportation of supplies.
- Safety equipment, including gloves, goggles, and masks for handling chemicals.

6. For a Jewellery Boutique:

- Jewellery organizers and displays to keep precious pieces organized.
- Gift boxes and packaging materials for a delightful presentation.
- Jewellery cleaning kits and solutions to maintain the beauty of accessories.
- Personalized jewellery-making kits containing

supplies like beads, enabling customers to design their own unique pieces.

- Jewellery-making tools and equipment, such as pliers, wire cutters, and bead boards.

7. For a Restaurant:

- Locally sourced spices and seasonings for customers to recreate flavours at home.
- Specialty cooking oils or vinegars that add unique touches to dishes.

8. For a Travel Agency:

- Travel accessories like luggage tags and passport holders for convenient identification.
- Travel-sized toiletries and personal care products for hassle-free packing.
- Travel guides and language phrasebooks to assist with trip planning and language learning

9. For a Home Security Company:

- Security cameras and monitoring systems for enhanced safety.
- Smart door locks and security alarms for peace of mind.
- Safety deposit boxes or home safes for secure storage.

10. For a Coffee Farmer:

- Coffee grinders and brewing equipment for the ultimate coffee experience.
- Coffee flavour syrups and additives to customize beverages. This is to include Additives like chocolate powder, cinnamon, or flavoured powders to provide unique twists to coffee creations, natural sweeteners like honey or agave syrup as alternatives to traditional sugar and a variety of flavoured syrups, including classics like vanilla, caramel, or hazelnut, to enhance the taste of coffee beverages.
- Curated coffee subscription services offering a selection of freshly roasted beans delivered directly to customers' doors.
- Gift boxes featuring different coffee blends or single-origin coffees, accompanied by tasting notes or brewing recommendations.
- DIY Organic Garden Kit that provide organic seeds, soil, and instructions for customers to grow their own coffee plants at home, educational materials explaining the coffee cultivation process, from seed to harvest, and the necessary care for coffee plants and additional supplies like planters, fertilizer, and pruning tools to support the growth of coffee plants.

11. For a Bicycle Repair Man

- Cycling apparel and accessories including performance cycling jerseys, shorts and protective gear such as helmets and gloves for safety.
- Bike repair and maintenance tools including tire levers, patch kits, and mini pumps for quick fixes of flat tires and lubricants, degreasers, and cleaning brushes for proper bike maintenance.

12. For a Food Delivery Service:

- Eco-friendly and biodegradable disposable cutlery made from sustainable materials.
- Portion control containers to aid in meal planning and preparation for customers.
- Cooking spices or condiments like sauces, dressings, or marinades to accompany different types of cuisine and Spice blends or seasoning packets that customers can use to recreate restaurant-quality flavours at home.

13. For a Natural Skincare Brand:

- Facial cleansing brushes or tools to promote gentle exfoliation and skin renewal.
- Natural bath and body products.
- Essential oils and aromatherapy diffusers.

- **DIY Bath and Body Product Kits:** Kits that include ingredients like essential oils, carrier oils, and botanical extracts, along with instructions, for customers to create their own bath bombs, soaps, or lotions, detailed recipes and guides for making personalized bath and body products at home, allowing customers to customize scents and ingredients according to their preferences and additional tools and packaging materials, such as moulds, labels, and containers, for a complete DIY experience.

A Guide To Multiple Streams Of Income

Stream #5: Capitalizing Your Space

Capitalizing your space is a lucrative income stream involving utilizing unused or underutilized space to generate extra cash. This can be anything from a photo studio to a nail booth. If you have an area that needs to be fully utilized, renting it out could be an excellent way to supplement your income.

For photographers, this could mean renting out your photo studio to other photographers when you're not using it. This way, you can earn income while keeping your gear and equipment in your studio, ensuring they're readily available when you need them. Similarly, a phone repair technician could rent out their booth or store to other tech businesses, such as a phone accessories retailer. Doing this can increase traffic and exposure to your business, leading to potential customers and new business opportunities.

Accountants can also use this strategy by renting their office space to local artists. This can be an excellent way to support the local arts community and earn extra cash simultaneously. You can offer commission-based sales on any artwork sold, which can be a win-win for everyone involved.

BONUS

Here are some creative ideas to make the most of your space:

1. Utilize Your Space for Retail Sales:

If you venture into Stream 2 or 3, consider dedicating part of your primary location as a retail store. This allows you to sell products that are related to your industry, providing customers with convenient access to items they may need all the while enhancing the overall customer experience.

2. Rent Out Your Bar or Similar Space for Hosting Events:

If you have a bar or similar space within your business, explore the possibility of renting it out for hosting events. This could include private parties, corporate gatherings, or special occasions. By offering your space as a venue, you can generate income from event rentals while leveraging your existing infrastructure.

3. Rent Out Your School or Classroom Space for Conferences and Workshops:

If you have a school or classroom space that is not fully utilized during weekends or off-seasons, consider renting it out to host conferences, workshops, or training sessions. Businesses and organizations are often in need of suitable venues for their events, and your space can provide a valuable solution while generating additional revenue.

A Guide To Multiple Streams Of Income | 18

4. Rent Out Your Private Workout Space for Fitness Classes or Boot Camps:

If you are a personal trainer with a private workout space, consider renting it out to other fitness professionals or instructors. This allows them to conduct their own fitness classes or boot camps, providing an opportunity for collaborative partnerships and increasing the utilization of your space.

5. Host Specialty Cooking Classes in Your Restaurant:

If you own a restaurant, leverage your culinary expertise by offering specialty cooking classes. When your business is closed, you can utilize your kitchen and dining area to provide hands-on cooking experiences for enthusiasts. This not only generates additional revenue but also enhances the reputation and visibility of your restaurant.

6. Offer Property Tours for Farm Owners:

If you are a farmer, consider offering access to your property for tours at an additional cost. This can attract visitors who are interested in learning about agricultural practices, farm life, or sustainable farming methods. By providing informative and engaging tours, you can diversify your income while showcasing your farm and educating the public.

7. Implement a embership or Subscription Model for Exclusive Access:

Explore the possibility of offering a membership or subscription model to provide exclusive access to your space. For instance, you can create a community garden space within your farm and offer monthly

subscriptions for individuals to cultivate their own produce. Similarly, photographers can pay a monthly fee for exclusive access to your photography studio on weekends. This approach not only generates recurring revenue but also fosters a sense of community and loyalty among your customers.

8. Lease Land Space for Billboards:

Depending on the location of your home or other properties, consider leasing land space to business owners for the installation of billboards. This provides a passive income stream without requiring significant involvement on your part. Ensure that you comply with local regulations and consider partnering with reputable advertising agencies or outdoor media companies.

9. Add Vending Machines to Your Space:

Increase convenience and generate additional income by installing vending machines in your business space. Offer snacks, beverages, or other products that align with your industry or cater to the needs of your customers. This self-service approach allows for 24/7 availability and can supplement your primary offerings.

10. Incorporate Pay-for Use Game Boxes in Your Space:

Create an engaging and interactive experience by incorporating pay-for-use game boxes in your business space. These can include arcade machines, video game consoles, or tabletop games. Customers can enjoy entertainment while you earn revenue from game usage fees.

Stream #6: Personalized Swag & Clothes

Creating personalized branding and apparel is a great way to showcase your individuality and attract new clients. Whether you're a photographer, farmer, nail technician, or phone repair technician, you can use your creativity to design and sell products that align with your brand and personality.

For example, photographers can offer photobooks with their custom logos, keychains, and mugs with their unique designs. Farmers can create shirts with catchy slogans like "Growing with Purpose" or "From the Fields with Love," that showcase their brand and love for farming. Nail technicians can sell branded manicure sets or aprons with their logo. Phone repair technicians can offer phone cases with their custom design, or even branded t-shirts.

Having a variety of personalized products can add an extra income stream and serve as a marketing tool for your business. By wearing or using these items, you can promote your brand and create a memorable impression on your clients, customers, and colleagues.

Stream #7: Social Media

Social media is a platform that provides limitless opportunities for professionals from various backgrounds. It's an effective way to reach a massive audience and expand your brand. Utilizing social media platforms like Instagram, Facebook, and Twitter is a great way to interact with your followers and showcase your work. You can post pictures, videos, or live streams of your work and engage with your followers. This creates a sense of community and trust between you and your followers, making promoting your products and services easier.

For example, photographers can showcase their latest shoots, post behind-the-scenes footage, and share their work process. Farmers can post pictures of their crops and share tips and tricks for growing crops. Phone repair technicians can post tutorials on how to repair various gadgets and offer repair services. The possibilities are endless, and with the right strategy, you can use social media to your advantage and supplement your income.

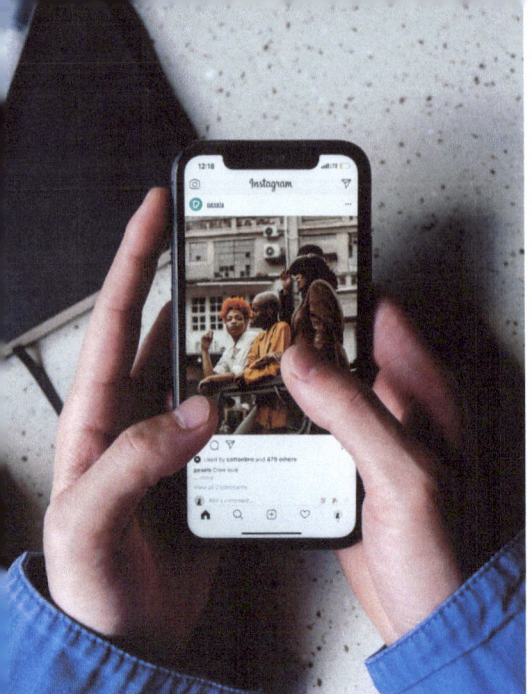

BONUS

Here are some ways to maximize your social media presence for business growth:

1. Create, Manage, and Execute Effective Ad Campaigns: Platforms like Facebook, Instagram, and LinkedIn offer robust advertising capabilities. Take advantage of their targeted ad options to reach your desired audience effectively. By creating well-crafted ad campaigns, you can increase brand visibility, drive traffic to your products or services, and ultimately boost sales.

2. Set Up an Online Shop on Social Media Platforms: Many social media platforms now provide features that allow you to set up an online shop directly within your profile. Utilize these e-commerce capabilities to provide customers with a seamless shopping experience. By offering your products for sale on social media, you provide an additional channel for potential customers to discover and purchase from you.

3. Provide Reviews and Collaborate with Brands: Sharing reviews of the products or services you use in your work can benefit your business in multiple ways. Not only does it drive additional traffic to your social media page, but it can also attract the attention of brands looking for influential partners. Through successful brand partnerships, you can secure lucrative collaborations, sponsorships, or endorsements that further boost your revenue.

4. **Manage Social Media Accounts and Offer Guidance:** Once you have developed a strong social media presence and gained expertise in managing your own accounts, consider offering your services to manage the social media accounts of others in your field. Many businesses and individuals are willing to pay for professional assistance with content creation, engagement strategies, and growth tactics. Additionally, you can create and offer a comprehensive guide on content creation, engagement, and growth strategies to help others improve their social media presence.

5. **Join Affiliate Programs and Promote Products or Services:** Affiliate marketing is a powerful way to earn passive income through your social media platforms. Join relevant affiliate programs and promote products or services that align with your brand and target audience. By sharing unique affiliate links, you can earn a commission for each sale or referral made through your link. Select reputable affiliate programs and focus on products or services that resonate with your followers to maximize your success

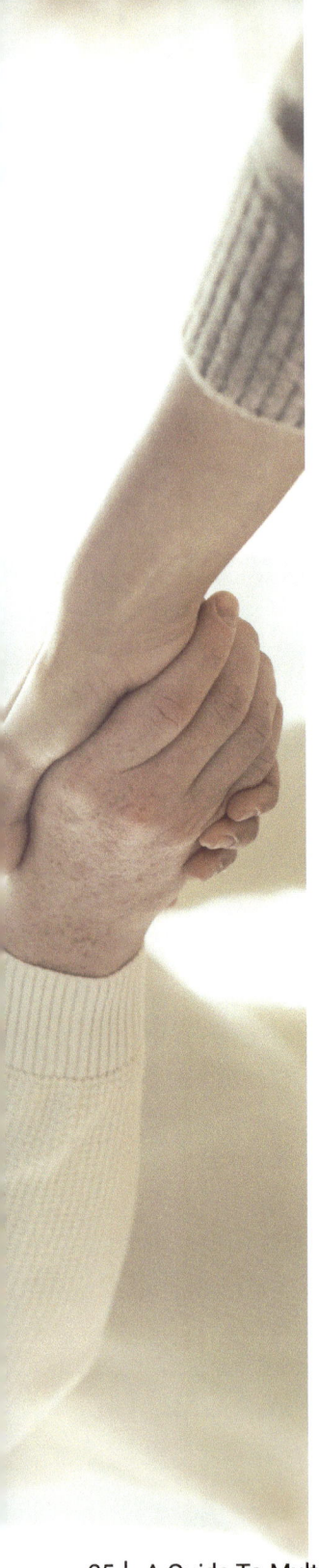

Stream #8:
Brand Partnership

Collaborating with other businesses or brands can be a strategic way for professionals to boost their income and grow their brand. By joining complementary brands, professionals can leverage each other's strengths, reach new audiences, and offer new, innovative products and services.

For instance, a photographer can offer a special bundle deal in partnership with a camera brand, providing clients with not just a photography service but also a high-quality camera to capture memories. A nail technician can join forces with a jewelry brand to create unique nail art that doubles as wearable jewelry. A phone repair technician can collaborate with a tech store to offer a complete phone repair and upgrade solution. A farmer can work with a government agency that promotes and supports farming to provide unique and sustainable products. An accountant can team up with a textbook brand to offer a study package that includes accounting guidance and recommended study materials.

Partnerships of this nature can bring a new level of credibility and exposure to the professionals, increasing their client base and, ultimately, their income. It's a win-win situation for all parties involved, as it helps both brands grow and reach their goals.

Bonus Streams to Earn More Money:

1. Renting out Property:

Renting out a property such as a spare room, an apartment, or a vacation home can provide a steady stream of passive income. This can be done through Airbnb, VRBO, or Booking.com.

2. Investing in Stocks, Bonds, or Mutual Funds:

Investing in the stock market, bonds, or mutual funds can provide a potential for high returns, although it also comes with risks. It is essential to consult a financial advisor and do proper research before making any investment decisions.

3. Selling Products or Services Online:

Selling products or services through an e-commerce platform, such as Amazon, Etsy, or Shopify, can reach a wider audience and increase sales.

4. Freelance Work:

Freelancing allows individuals to offer their skills and services to clients worldwide without being tied to a traditional 9-5 job. Freelancers can find work through Upwork, Fiverr, or Freelancer platforms.

5. Consulting or Coaching:

Sharing expertise and knowledge through consulting or coaching can provide additional income. This can be done by offering one-on-one sessions, workshops, or courses.

6. **Gigs through Platforms like Fiverr, Upwork, or TaskRabbit:**
Participating in short-term, project-based work through platforms such as Fiverr, Upwork, or TaskRabbit can provide a flexible source of income.

7. **Peer-to-Peer Lending:**
Peer-to-peer lending allows individuals to earn returns on investments by lending money directly to individuals or small businesses. This can be done through platforms such as Lending Club or Prosper.

8. **Franchise or License Your Business Model:**
If you have a successful business model, consider franchising or licensing it to others. This allows you to expand your brand presence and generate income through franchise fees or licensing royalties.

9. **Mobility:**
Bring Your Services to Your Clients' Doorsteps: If you are in industries such as food service, beauty, agriculture, car detailing, or other mobile-friendly businesses, create mobile units that bring your services directly to clients' homes. This provides convenience and personalized experiences, attracting more customers and increasing your earning potential.

10. **Car Advertising:**
Turn your vehicle into a moving advertisement by partnering with companies that pay for car wraps or decals. This passive income stream utilizes your daily commute to generate extra cash.

11. **Mobile Notary:**
Offer mobile notary services, catering to individuals and businesses in need of notarization services outside of traditional office hours or locations. This flexible service can be in high demand and allow you to charge premium rates for your expertise.

Jamaican Bonus Business Ideas:

Jamaica is not only known for its beautiful beaches and vibrant culture but also presents various opportunities for entrepreneurs to tap into unique business ideas. In this chapter, we explore a range of bonus business ideas that showcase the diverse potential of the Jamaican market.

1. Leasing Billboard Space to Entrepreneurs:

Utilize prime locations by leasing billboard space to entrepreneurs for advertising their products or services. This creates a win-win situation, as you generate income while supporting local businesses in reaching their target audience.

2. Tour Guide: Eco-Tourism & Nature Excursion:

With Jamaica's breathtaking natural landscapes and rich biodiversity, there is ample opportunity to offer eco-tourism and nature excursions. Become a knowledgeable tour guide, showcasing the island's unique flora, fauna, and sustainable practices to eco-conscious travellers.

3. Transportation Service:

Provide transportation services, such as shuttle buses or private car rentals, catering to tourists and locals alike. Offering reliable, comfortable, and convenient transportation options can be a lucrative business venture.

Distribution: Reverse the distribution process by acting as a distributor for foreign products in Jamaica. Identify popular international brands or products that are not readily available on the island and bring them to the local market, catering to the demand of Jamaican consumers.

4. Wellness Retreats:
Capitalize on Jamaica's serene environment and wellness culture by organizing wellness retreats. Provide a sanctuary for individuals seeking relaxation, rejuvenation, and holistic healing experiences, incorporating yoga, meditation, spa treatments, and nutritious cuisine.

5. Local Product Distribution:
Act as a distributor for local Jamaican products overseas, showcasing the country's vibrant arts and crafts, specialty foods, spices, and other unique items. Connect local artisans and craftspeople with customers worldwide through an online marketplace.

6. Overseas Product

7. Online Marketplace

for Local Artisans: Create an online platform that allows local artisans and craftspeople to showcase and sell their products to a global customer base. Offer authentic Jamaican goods, such as handmade dutch pots, ratchet knives, traditional clothing, and artwork, connecting buyers with the country's rich cultural heritage.

8. Beach Equipment

Rental: Cater to tourists visiting Jamaica's stunning beaches by offering equipment rentals. Provide items like clear kayaks, snorkeling gear, beach umbrellas, and loungers, ensuring visitors have a memorable and enjoyable beach experience.

9. Special Occasion

Wear Rental: Tap into the growing trend of destination weddings and photoshoots by offering rental services for special occasion wear. Provide tourists with a range of elegant and stylish outfits, enabling them to capture stunning memories against Jamaica's scenic backdrop.

10. Bodyguard or Personal Security Services:

Ensure the safety and security of high-profile individuals, tourists, or event attendees by offering bodyguard or personal security services. This specialized service can provide peace of mind and protection in various situations.

11. **Rent Event Décor:** Create a business around event décor rentals, catering to weddings, corporate events, and private parties. Offer a wide range of themes, styles, and decorative items to transform venues into memorable and visually appealing spaces.

12. **Rent Mobile Photo Booth:** Capitalize on the popularity of photo booths by offering mobile photo booth rentals for events. Provide a fun and interactive experience, complete with props and custom backdrops, allowing guests to capture and share their memorable moments.

13. **Self-Service Coin-Operated Laundry:** Address the practical needs of residents and tourists by establishing self-service coin-operated laundry facilities. Offer a convenient and affordable solution for individuals looking to launder their clothes while enjoying their time in Jamaica.

Bonus Section:
Tools for Entrepreneurs:

As an entrepreneur, leveraging the right tools can greatly enhance your productivity, organization, and overall success. By utilizing these tools, you can effectively manage various aspects of your business, from marketing and communication to finance and productivity. Choose the tools that align with your specific needs and goals, and leverage their features to optimize your entrepreneurial endeavours.

- **Asana:** Asana is a project management tool that helps teams stay organized and collaborate on projects. It's free for up to 15 team members, with paid plans starting at $9.99/month.

- **Airtable:** Airtable is a flexible database tool that combines the power of spreadsheets with the ability to organize data into tables, views, and forms. It's free for up to 1200 records, with paid plans starting at $10/month.

- **Slack:** Slack is a communication platform that makes communicating and collaborating with team members easy. It's free for small teams, with paid plans starting at $6.67/month.

- **Flodesk:** Flodesk is an email marketing tool that allows you to create and send beautiful, professional emails. It offers a 30-day free trial, with paid plans starting at $19/month

- **Structured:** Structured is a business management tool that streamlines operations and automates repetitive tasks. It's free for up to 2 users, with paid plans starting at $29/month

- **Bench Accounting:** Bench Accounting is an online bookkeeping service that provides real-time financial data, insights, and reports. It offers a free trial, with paid plans starting at $139/month.

Canva: Canva is a graphic design tool that makes it easy to create professional-looking designs, even if you have yet to gain design experience. It's free, with paid plans starting at $12.95/month.

Later.com: Later is a social media management tool that allows you to plan, schedule, and publish content across multiple platforms. It's free for up to 30 posts per platform, with paid plans starting at $19/month.

Upwork: Upwork is a platform that connects freelancers with clients for various projects, from writing to graphic design to programming. It's free for freelancers, with clients charged a fee for each project.

Mailchimp: Mailchimp is an email marketing platform that allows you to create, automate, and analyse email campaigns. It offers a free plan with limited features, while paid plans start at $9.99/month, offering more advanced functionality.

Hootsuite: Hootsuite is a social media management tool that enables you to schedule and manage your social media content across multiple platforms. It offers a free plan for individual users, with paid plans starting at $29/month for more extensive features and team collaboration.

Charguel: Charguel is an online invoicing and billing software that helps you create and manage professional invoices, track payments, and handle billing tasks. It offers a free plan for up to three clients, with paid plans starting at $15/month for larger businesses.

Dashlane: Dashlane is a password management tool that securely stores and autofills your passwords across various websites and apps. It offers a free plan with limited features, while paid plans start at $3.33/month, providing additional security and convenience.

- **Zapier:** Zapier is an automation tool that connects different apps and platforms, allowing you to automate workflows and streamline repetitive tasks. It offers a free plan with basic automation capabilities, while paid plans start at $19.99/month for more complex integrations.

- **Final Cut Pro:** Final Cut Pro is a professional video editing software designed for filmmakers and video creators. It provides advanced editing tools, effects, and post-production features. Final Cut Pro is available for a one-time purchase at $299.99, offering powerful capabilities for creating high-quality videos.

www.ingramcontent.com/pod-product-compliance
Lightning Source LLC
Chambersburg PA
CBHW041943240526
45473CB00033B/486